Poetic Ditherings- Observations, Philosophies and Attempts at Wisdom

Luke Mayo

Presentation by *BookLeaf Publishing*

Web: www.bookleafpub.com

E-mail: info@bookleafpub.com

ISBN: 978939575616

First edition 2022

DEDICATION

This book is dedicated to everyone who creates art in any and every form, and to everyone who enjoys it.

ACKNOWLEDGEMENT

There are so many people to whom I owe a debt
of thanks for their positive impact on my life. I
attempt to list a few of them here.

The charities I've worked and volunteered for, of
whom there are far too many to mention. The
experiences I've had with you all are invaluable
as a source of poetic inspiration.

The University of Suffolk and its English
Department, for instilling and developing in me
a love of poetry.

Lastly, but not leastly, my family. It sounds
cliched to say that I couldn't have done it
without you, but it's fundamentally true.

Thank you all.

PREFACE

Everyone, as they live life, garners a level of
experience, wisdom and perception on what they
see around them. How we channel that
information is different for each one of us.

These poems are the way in which I've chosen to
channel my experiences in life. I hope you enjoy
them.

A Diarist's Torments

Dear Diary
With these words
I chronicle this day
The things I have seen
The deeds I have done

I commit to paper
This woeful
Gut wrenching
Soul destroying
Hopeless day

I set in ink
This fateful day
When my life changed
From being ordinary
To being cast into shadows
Despair
Loneliness

Every day
I have written of so far
Has been normal
Fairly pleasant
Perhaps a tad dull
But otherwise enjoyably unnoticeable

But now
I write about today
It has been a monumental day
For all the wrong reasons

All the stability that I hold so dear
It has been uprooted and discarded
To be replaced with uncertainty and fear
The path I walk
Once alight with sunshine
Is now dampened by rain
Heralding the oncoming storm

What words will I write tomorrow?
Will they be words touched by the light of hope?
Or will they be words drawn from a heart
plunged further into darkness?

A Lonely Room

By the ticking of the clock
The days slowly pass by
By the ticking of the clock
No one can hear me cry
By the ticking of the clock
I lie all on my own
By the ticking of the clock
My heart turns into stone

For a long time now
I've been lying on this hospital bed
I can't remember how long it's been
But I no longer care

All I care about
Is my love for my friends
The people I once shared my life with

The times we shared
They mean everything to me
Did they matter to my friends?
I fear not
For they seem to have forgotten me

I lie here paralysed

Day after day
Not one visitor enters the room
With each tick of the clock
My hopes die away
That we may be reunited

By the ticking of the clock
My life is slipping past
By the ticking of the clock
I'm going nowhere fast
By the ticking of the clock
I wish my friends were here
By the ticking of the clock
No friends can be found here

I Journey On

To overpower all my foes
To earn some peace after my woes
To find the highs after the lows
I journey on

To show the world how much I've grown
To show I've come into my own
To earn my place upon life's throne
I journey on

For all the friends whose love is clear
Who helped me overcome each fear
Who in my heart I hold so dear
I journey on

As for the folks who put me down
Who robbed my smile and made me frown
To prove to them that I'm no clown
I journey on

No matter what the journey's length
I'll develop all my strength
There is no power or worldly wrath
That can dissuade me from my path

This wacky life of mine, it brings
The chance for me to do good things
Until those good things have been done
I will not think the battle won

My legacy
I hope will be
Brighter places
Happier faces

If this is so
Then joy I'll know
I'll never die
Just watch me fly

Until You Came

All was well
Until you came

My life was happy
Until you came

I had everything I wanted
Until you came

There was once a time
When my heart was filled with joy
I lived each day
With a smile on my face
No matter what may occur
I could face it
For there was strength in me

But then you appeared
Like a bolt of lightning across the sky

That's when my life changed

You took my life
And turned it upside down
You paralysed me

And sucked the life from me

The strength and joy I once knew
Is now gone
Because of you

You captivated me
With your excitement
You blinded me
With your charisma
Then you ruined me
With your selfish arrogance

Now you've gone
And you took my soul with you

I had a life to be proud of
Until you came

The Spirit of Nature

Do you know the Spirit of Nature?
Have you felt his presence?
Have you seen his ways?
Have you heard him speak?

I have

He is in the cool evening breeze
He is in the sounds of the woodland glen
He is in the river that flows past the trees

He is everywhere

He does not always make himself known
But when he does
He is a friend to all who respect him
And seek to learn from his wisdom

He is as old as the Earth
And has experienced much
He is kind and benevolent
But will unleash his wrath
Upon those who deserve it
He seeks to be one with us

And for harmony to be maintained

Not everyone knows the Spirit
But how blessed are those that do

The Precipice and the Sky

My vision stretches for miles around
Yet somehow it seems to stop dead in front of
my eyes
So little to see
So much to take in

The road stops here
The cliff edge has been reached
I'm sat on a rock
I'm looking at what lies beneath me

A treacherous drop
Death lies at the end
Vicious rocks
Jagged and deadly
One thing I know
There's no life down there

The precipice in its entirety is frightful to behold
For some reason it entices me
It draws me in and welcomes me

It's only when I look up that my vision changes

The sky

So deep and clear
The sun
Its light and warmth embracing everything it
meets
The birds
Singing for joy and delighting in the power of
flight

The funny thing is
The sky doesn't stop
It goes on for ever
Endless in its inspiration

The opposite of the cliff edge

If death and despair lies below me
Life and hope well and truly stands above me

What an extraordinary vision
Up and down
Above and beneath
Hope and despair
Even at the end of the road
There are still discoveries and achievements
They can still be found if you know where to
look

It's never too late to do that

The Time For Creativity

The day is over
The sun has set
The moon and stars have taken their place in the
sky

The world is quiet
Peacefully sleeping
Patiently waiting for tomorrow to come

But my mind is far from resting

For this time of quiet
It's my time for productivity

I have the freedom to do anything
I can create worlds of imagination
Make beautiful music
Construct visual sights of wonder
Solve the mysteries of the universe

My daily life is so busy
That I have little time for creative pursuits
That's what the night time is there for

When some choose to sleep
I choose to create

The End

We take each day for granted
Using them
Wasting them
Frittering them away
Devoting our time to nothing much at all

Do we ever wonder:
Which day will be our last?
Could it be next year?
Next month?
Next week?
Tomorrow?
Today?

At the back of our minds
We are all aware
That we are inching closer
To the edge of a precipice
But we have no idea
When that precipice will be reached

What memory will we leave behind?
What will the others say when we are gone?
Will they mourn?

Rejoice?
Curse?

What if no one remembers us?

We are unique in how we spend our time
But we are united in that our time is limited

The Hearts of Many

I have had many partners
And shared my heart with vast numbers

Over the course of my life
People have stood by my side
And come with me on adventures
We have laughed, loved and lost together
And we have bonded a great deal

But that bond
Never lasts for long

The people I am with
Come and go
As the day turns to night
As the seasons change
As life begins and ends

How I long
To stay with someone
And keep to their side
Through thick and thin
Overcoming all obstacles
To remain together

I have appeared and vanished
From the hearts of many
What I want more than anything
Is a permanent place
In the heart of one

Responding to Downturns

Blunders
They occur regularly
Mistakes
Everyone makes them
Accidents
They always happen

How do we respond
When we fall to the ground?
By getting back up

Ultimately
It matters not what happens
What matters
Is how we deal with it

Setbacks
They do not define us
How we approach them does

Do we remain stuck
In our dark world of self pity?
Or do we build a ladder
Grow wings
Find any other solution

To find our way out?

Responding to downturns
We are all united
In that we must do this one thing
What separates us
Is how we sort them out

Music Soothes the Soul

My savaged mind
It twists and turns in anguish
My pained soul
It is battered and bruised each day
My broken heart
It howls at the darkness and torment

What tools can I use
To calm the storm that rages within?

Music

Its melodies sweep over me
Taking hold of the pain inside
And out of my pain grows a smile
As the torment slowly melts away
All thanks to the music which captivates my
entire being

Music
How can I dismiss it?
Ignore it?
Abandon it?
It has moved me so deeply
Changed me so dramatically

Helped me so tremendously

Once music has spoken to your heart
Resonated with it
Helped you to forget the pain
There's no going back

The power of music
Don't resist it
Embrace it

Meaningless Pain

We search for meaning in this life
A reason behind all the strife
Before long, we become aware
We search for something that's not there

Every day
Bad things happen
Good people suffer
Wicked people thrive
Disasters occur
Lives are ruined
And we wonder why

What if
There's no reason for it all?
What if
All the bad things are pure chance?
What if
We have no control over our dark fate?

There is no meaning for our pain
Which visits us time and again
These bad things happen randomly
With no way for us to be free

No matter how hard we try
We cannot escape the suffering
We furiously question why fate has chosen us
But no answer can be found

All we can do
Is use the pain to grow stronger
Persevere through the torment
To live constructive lives
And be compassionate towards other sufferers
For we are united in our maladies

Reasons for pain may not exist
But strength is found when we resist
Facing the darkness helps us grow
And thus, with courage, on we go

Empty Achievements

We yearn for success
And the tiniest crumb of fame
We push ourselves to the limit
To achieve our goals

Then we achieve them
And we stand in the midst of what we've done
And we look back on our lives
And we ask ourselves:
Was it worth it?

We toiled away
Day and night
Our minds overwhelmed
Crying out in pain
Friends turning away
Sanity slowly diminishing
All to gain what we wanted so badly

What are we willing to lose
To get what we want?
What lengths will we go to
In order to achieve our heart's desire
Where do we draw the line
Between passion and foolhardiness?

Is getting what we want
Worth losing the good we have?

Intuition

What is this thing
That guides me through life?

Intuition?
Conscience?
Wisdom?
Common sense?

Whatever its name
I am grateful for it
For it informs my every decision
And keeps me tight to the right path
As I journey through each day

As I travel down life's path
I will often encounter
A fork in the road

Which way do I turn?

This consciousness in me
This voice of wisdom
It has the answer

Whenever I'm in a bind

And unsure of what to do
I listen to the voice
And all turns out well

Conversations with the Departed

You've departed this life
"I shall not completely die"
No trace of you remains
"My memory lives on"
How can I survive without you?
"Hold on to our love"

The folks we love
They all depart
But their love stays
Within our heart

I'll think of you every day
"Honour me with your life"
I'll never forget the impact you've had
"May our love inspire you to greatness"
You'll never lose your place in my life
"It's an honour to have been yours"

The end of life
Leads love to grief
But thankfully
This pain is brief

I hope you've found peace now
"I hope you do good with your life"
I hope you're in a good place
"I hope your days to come are joyous"
I hope we meet again somehow
"I look forward to reuniting with you"

In life, in death
May love remain
Along with hope
We'll meet again

Needing a Label

Every day goes by
Every place we go
Every person we meet

Countless members of humanity
We walk past them briefly
It takes a few seconds
The time it takes to tell their life story

Everyone we pass by
Everything about them is hidden from us
Their identity
Their backstory
Their emotions
Their soul

This doesn't stop us
Judgements are made
Stories are written
Characters are formed
Fates are sealed

Every possible tic
Every possible neurosis

Every possible emotion
We diagnose and offer a prognosis
No second glances required
Our own perception is all that counts

Little do we realise
The same is done to us by those we judge

The people whose existence we set in stone
They too choose a stone for us
This is what humans do to each other
We entrap each other with a label

Peculiar An-Tics

A smack of the lips
A crack of the knuckles
A bounce of the legs
A twitch of the eyes

We all have our personal habits
They're unique to us
We reserve them for certain situations
Stress
Boredom
Irritation

We barely realise we do them
They're entirely unconscious

There's one time we immediately recognise
them
That's when we observe them in others
The nail shewing
The eye rolling
The inpatient sighs

We can ignore our own habit
But we're incapable of doing the same for others
Then they are magnified and scrutinised

The centrepiece of existence

We are already riddled with frustration
It's compounded by the observation of those
habits
Why can't we leave others to it?
Why can't we focus on ourselves?

Will we ever learn?

The Rain Outside

Outside looking in
The rain descends
What a lonely place
Cold
Wet
Exposed

Far better to be inside looking out

It's safer inside
Warmer
Calmer

Being alone isn't lonely in here
It's comforting to listen to the rain
The sound of patter against the roof
The sight of the vibrant green nature outside
The smell of rejuvenated soil

Rainy days can be sad when you're stuck out in
them
But they're not so bad when observed from
within

There's space to breathe

To notice
To take stock
To make the plans

The sun shines
The clouds congregate
The rain comes down
Then the sun emerges again

The cycle of the sky has always been so
Long may the rain reign

Dampening the Chaos

The emotions blaze within me
Scorching
Burning
Overwhelming

Every waking moment
Wherever I go
Whoever I'm with
Whenever I close my eyes
Those emotions still blaze

Running riot
No boundaries
Every whim pursued
I am powerless

"Let me see what I can prescribe"

A note from the doctor
A bag over the counter
A pill a day

The storm subsides
The rain eases off
The winds slow down

All that remains is a foggy blur

The chaos is no more
All because of a humble pill
Each day the pill is taken
Exactly the same as the previous day
And the following day will also match

The pill dampens the chaos

The Dilemma of Calling Time

We want the dream job
We spend our days searching
Application after application
Endless rejections
We want the job
But we need the money
Do we hold out?
Or do we settle for something else?

The relationship is on the rocks
Years of invested emotion at stake
So much water under the bridge
We want it to work out
But we see no way
Do we keep trying?
Or do we walk away?

Choosing to hold on
Choosing to let go
Choosing to forge ahead
Choosing to turn back

This is one of life's hardest decisions
We don't want failure

We want satisfaction
But what if we can't find it?
What do we do then?

When do we stop trying?

Waiting Room

Sat in a chair
Blank walls
Lino floors
Clinical overtones

Waiting for those elusive words
"The doctor will see you now"

Such a plain room to wait in
Yet such a broad range of people pass through
A holding pen for humanity

Extroverts
Introverts
Youth
Elderly
Artists
Scientists

So many different people
United in their need for support

We are called for our appointment
We lay ourselves bare
We expose our vulnerabilities

We hope to get better

A horde of different people
Together as one in the waiting room